*

TASTING THE STARS

TASTING THE *Stars*

By Tina Gonçalves

Tasting the Stars
Sensuous & Contemplative Poetry

© Copyright Tina Gonçalves, 2020

All rights reserved. No part of this publication may be reproduced or transmitted in any form or by any means, including photocopying, recording, or other electronic or mechanical methods, without the prior written permission of the author.

This writing may be shared on all social platforms if credit is attributed to the author and the book title is referenced @alya.rising / Tina Gonçalves / Tasting the Stars

ISBN: 978-0-646-81981-5 / Poetry, Spirituality

Published 2020 by Tina Gonçalves
https://tinagoncalves.com

Mentoring:

David Caddy, Tears in the Fence
https://tearsinthefence.com/

Scott MacMillan, Grammar Factory
https://grammarfactory.com/

Typesetting & Design:
Tina Gonçalves

*dedicated lovingly
to the great dance
between us
all*

List of Poems

Part One

Inhale

precipice
wildflower love

—

Dharamshala

—

freedom in the wild
jewel of sea

—

dear one

—

heart light
equinox
this touch of you

List of Poems

the first note

cinnamon

desire Is

taken

the rose

-

silk

fullness

melting Devi

-

alchemical We

honey gold

hymn to Shiva

keep me at the gate

involution

List of Poems

Part Two
Exhale

bow

-

Kali Ma
anoint me
dreams I did
breathe now
beingness

-

soft
echo

-

see
seed
circle
inlakesh

List of Poems

⁃

bless

I am

⁃

rise

alchemy

creation

em cima da mesa

Love

⁃

temple keeper

Philae

Maat

⁃

Sahara

raining Light

destination nil

when I

⁃

*

"A metaphor is not an ornament.
It is an organ of perception."

–Neil Postman

*

Part One

Inhale

precipice

a spirit rises
taking to this sea   soaring

these wings
unseen immutable Grace

gathering in flight
to a world unknown
craved for

the spirit glides
along the precipice

sharp-eyed
hunting for discovery

wildflower love

this state of Heart is not a destination
it cannot be anywhere
but within

here
I listen for a fragrance of stillness
        wait for silence to emerge

the Mountain knows...

flowers still bend toward the sun
the ants go about their day

weeds and the wild   flourish

nature goes on
        eating itself and making love

        as I pause

*

Awe

for every atom

in this strange sea of existence

this power that brings beauty into being

Dharamshala

butterflies of the Kangra
                        set adrift

these white spells of light
        rising   tiny flutters

caressing the edge of the world
their oblivion unknown

here
        folded in this nuance of hope

        delicate as   *silk*
                        gold embers

            making love

                        to the void

here

        and there

            where monks burn

their wings offered in sacrifice for freedom

their ashes

      set adrift

as these butterflies

    continue

        to rise

*

you were born
wild and free

nothing can
bind you

*

freedom in the wild

freedom in the wild
I have everything   I have
nothing

like air, the archetype of emptiness fills me
makes me whole

here I have lipstick   responsibility

I wear leather like an attitude
hot with impatience

it masks my simmering
silent fury

a place where lines are forged
and vastness is born

jewel of sea

a jewel of sea   s h i m m e r i n g
crowned by the glory of sun
beckons skin

every molecule   rich with providence
promises

mountains of swell   mighty, lulling

      liquid-light submersed
silent

        white

breathless

        tumbling...

*

providence

*she's in our breath
making love to our cells*

bless
*

lost...
move my soul

        pause
            wait

                *

                   listen...

dear one

you take me in your hand
and breathe me

guide me far
to the bluest seas

a deep embrace in
and a   l o n g   exhale

so full, so sweet
I can die in the stillness
between you

*

for so long I felt it guide me and end me
... and ignite the oil in this offering

*

where you came

heart light

wrapped in warm circles
angel walking

you gather me
      in Heart Light

a soft-eyed embrace

in the deep
suspended time   *stirring awake*

equinox

an equinox
standing with you

these pinks and blue
blending the edges of sky
and this salty wind in the wild, rolling

we, wrapped beneath this shawl of mine
our skin shimmering

our breath cooed by moon rays
on incandescent sea

our scent drawing us in
falling

this touch of you

this touch of you
so smooth on my wings

you are silk threaded through essence
freedom melded with Love

open to tantalise

you hold these strands of me quietly
weaving my core in your embrace

drinking the flame
silence

*

far above
music leaves pulse

the first note

the first note was light
the second, skin

pure, unadulterated
fragrant, all knowing trace
captivated by the giving in

delight of the ages
woven sound

cinnamon

I can see myself there

with sunlight glitter
and cinnamon cream

purely to seduce

delight in every ray
tingling to the tune of your lips

desire Is

dancing
up the ladder to Sky
and down the fabric of Ma

She implodes now
inside the tenderness of my heart
so wet here   and impermanent

taken

you take me in

you till the ground
gather my soil

softly   comforting

you take me In

where each breath allows
a sacrifice to this moment

and I die
in the expansion   and live

you take me   in

to hear the heartbeat   where
irrefutable Love
Is

the rose

you wait for the quiver   knowing
    and pause

close to my skin

savouring each breath   drinking me in

no words
just the pause   of sense

and the presence
of you

mingled inside my heart
    desire ablaze

closenesschest on my chest
            you enter

    so deep into the pleasure

enveloped by this rose
tasting the stars

*

lover
all I ask is
that you savour me

silk

if you could trace a line
along my thigh

you'd find me there
softer than silk

aching for you

fullness

I look across at you
brazen gaze   smiling

imagining
the fullness of you

falling senseless

to these curves along my lips
dripping fire

melting Devi

warm I said
fire in the hearth of my belly

an ember astride
as freedom arrives

h o w l i n g
as I melt, to see you
in this vital light

sacred here
spread along an infinite line

home

and now the quiet
soulful resting
skin on skin
embrace

*

alchemical We

soma and seed
stirring

gentle

fathomless
wonder cloaked

gold

held inside
the You of I

the alchemical We
awakening

honey gold

honey gold, liquid eyes
radiating ancient Sun

I can hold the moment
stretching time with your smile

and die there awake
awash, bathed in eternity

hymn to Shiva

nothing compares
Shiva
to the pillar of You

      and I
emblazoned with your light

birthing stars

keep me at the gate

keep me
at the gate of your Heart

lest I enter unworthy
of knowing your Light

take me in your Sun

burn my existence
until only You remain

involution

a million stars, shining as One

I am the lock and the key
and the keeper by the gate

an Infinity of worlds

a dot far below
the quintessence of Life holds

fluid of Eternity

Love, the unbending
longing for the Sun

Part Two

Exhale

bow

I bow to you Love

for allowing me
to rest here

fully
as I am

to honour   you
exactly
     as you are

here we step my love

       * * *

where there are no rules, no guides
but the strength of our knowing beyond fear

Kali Ma

and so it was
Her presence mighty

not without invocation she came
with her Truth claim

anoint me

one can't fail Love
she simply presents the gate

still, I know I'm too much
for the average or brave

so I ask you…

>*anoint me*
>
>let me go
>*let me go to the milk lands*
>
>I want to leave
>*and dine eternally, with Rumi and Magdalene*

>…it's so obvious I don't belong here

dreams I did

one day tears
another day aches

each day separated
tore flesh from skin

I didn't know how to be
in a world without your integrity

my heart's trust shattered
hands smaller than my own

breathe now

slow the course
of story and verse

abide *here*
        allow

the wind has no resistance
nor the sun

in time   all is forgiven

all is worn down
to the fragrance of Light   and dust

beingness

it is time now
to undress

massage the pains you avoid

take a moment to feel
the unloved, the unwanted

notice who and what you reject

what do you see?

the touch of your presence
is a gift to yourself

*

*

on the sierra

a soft aimless wonder

moonrise,

waxing beside my dreams

soft

these folds in my sheets...

blue curves splayed seductively
by the memory of motion

a sillage of you and I
and the cadence of our waves

these folds in my sheets
still speak of the aches we share

the record of our love left in streams
of cotton and thread   made to caress

echo

an essence
of sage

sinking   surrender

diving in, forgiving
forgiving him for me

longing, listening
weaving

*

this effulgence of Life carries me
so delightfully

I become water

and He the wave
riding Surrender

*

see

your heart was always leading me

true   *strange arcs of time shining*
   I was so crazy   *humbled, infuriating!*

Love, it leads me still

seed

each day is a seed I enter and I await the light
revealing each nuance, new

let us meet here

where I can see your eyes ignite
catch the limitless

let's pour our love like the Sun
design an unfolding of gold

nourish our soil

I want to create with you
see

circle

we are the story of two lines   venturing
each to the other horizon

until one day we meet
in the autumn we embraced

as life moves away   *let them forget us*
Grace will have the final say

senile to the moment our eyes met
and I walked up to you
shining

Inlakesh

life continues   a recycled fabric of carbon
held conscious for moments

     there I sleep   *and wake*

the You of I punctuates
carves time
timeless

mirror of wings
Grace becoming

bless

this ode to simplicity
inherent   as I pause

in the paradise of this moment
delicately   cherishing

Here   This
paradise of my own two hands

I am

a goddess in the grass
softness beneath my feet

pure Sky
light dancing   above

I can hear myself shining

diving in this bliss
      I kiss the sparkles

gather stars like daisies
remember
I am

*

radiating within me
Light pours

*

ecstasy Is-ness

rise

observe the limits
my moon is crystal clear
she *shimmers*

aligned
        centre bound

inside   the light plays Her glory
.
.
.

                                      taste

        watch me

alchemy

I don't know how
nor why

I only know

Grace   *holds me together with Love*

and the fire of the Unknown   *forges me*

as gold
born   of the stars

creation

un-sung

            between the ocean
                  and He

beside my tears, gently
preparing

em cima da mesa

light caresses
opens Her

there is nothing to do
everything to be

petals
r e c e i v e

Love

there is nothing to resist

Love is the great
coalesence

here

Love moves my tongue
to taste beauty, form words
touch hearts
unravel

surrender to the bliss that pervades

this beauty and power
  of all that is soft
    and changing

*

temple keeper

dear one
meet my Heart

stand at Her gate

lend your might and temperance

be as the walls

help me create an island
where this softness knows no bounds

Philae

the stars above met stone

beneath my feet   remembering

my Heart   to Sky
cognisant in timeless knowing

you held my gaze
caught my tears to Philae

Light so pure
for eons

Maat

everything
is Love

everything

the great Truth
is indivisible
Beauty

Love is all there Is

everything is dissolving

Sahara

I am ready

everything has returned
to Light

the cosmic wind
and sand of the Eternal
has worn everything away

Joy remains

here
I surrender

to Eagles of time
beloved, delighted

in vastness
soft
        constancy
you can find me
bathing

raining Light

take a deep breath
let the world melt

within
this valley of the Heart

emerge as nectar

enter the Radiance

dissolving

        succulent

as water
raining Light

destination nil

rebel   there is no goal
there is nothing to attain, nor any where to go

the beating heart of this moment
Is timeless

dancing the finite
weaving the Infinite

                know your place...

coalesce with the compassion
and wisdom of this silence

Joy pervades

spinning

Shiva   *Shakti*
hiding as the Supreme
      you Are

when I

when I die
let these words
be flowers at your feet

know their fragrance as Love
take their essence as freedom
hear their silence as knowingness

know the great Innocence
of creation calls me home

light the camphor
unwavering

*

this universe knows our place in Infinity
come now, the language of unity beckons us

Dear Reader

dear one, I promise
when you call the Great Love
Love hears you and knows the sound of your name
your essence beyond time is a petal in the Heart of God
shining the Light behind all gods

to Love, you are an offering
a pattern of bliss, perfect as God breathes you
forges your hand, weaves these elements
shaking some, sending others to slumber for millennia upon millennia
now here you are, awake in a body of earth and water
alive with consciousness, moving slowly, shifting atoms about

dear one, I promise
when you call the Great Love
Love hears you and knows the sound of your name
Love is written in your essence

you are made of particles, vibrating
finding each other, melding to create new forms
inside you, outside you, beyond you
life is Living with and without you noticing
every day, the butterfly goes on as the heart aches

and you are being forged, simply to remember...
the god in your hands, the god in your heart
the god in this land, the god in this tree
the God in all things, and the Love

Author's Note

I began writing these poems as I became immersed in the pointings of non-dual tantra, after several years of contemplative practice.

There the mystery called me to embrace my inner experience exactly as it is. So I devoted myself to this and to the taste of truth, love and beauty at the source of all things... where every atom is merged as One; the unreal dissolves; our place in the fabric of creation becomes clear... in Love, as Love.

"Tasting the Stars" is a small collection of poems, like pirilampos (fireflies) illuminating this path for a brief moment; little vignettes of my senses smooshed with Grace.

I offer them to you in the spirit of beauty in which they arose.

With Love, Tina

April, 2020

What is Non-Duality & Tantra?

Non-duality refers to this: that which is undivided, permanent, and beyond form.

Paradigms of One-ness and the sacred interdependence of all things, permeate the spiritual landscape of human history; and within the esoteric heart of many world religions, shamanic and spiritual traditions there is a place where mystics arrive in the language of unity, that is Love.

This arising occurs when periods of deep practice and contemplation enter the 'pathless path' – where absolute commitment and surrender to a higher power is so strong, dogmas and norms are departed from, devotion becomes realisation, and separation dissolves as a complete, living embodiment of Love.

Tantra, in sanskrit means "to weave". Non-dual Tantra refers to an orientation of awareness that embraces the world of form and impermanence, to realise our true nature as that which is indivisible, unchanging and eternal.

In the words of Sri Ramakrishna, *"everything is sacred, exactly as it is"*.

About the Author

Tina Gonçalves is a simple devotee with honey in her heart. She offers meditation guidance and an invitation into the deep stillness of Life, embodied.

Drawn to the realm of poetic musings, archetypes and spiritual teachings as a child, she began a practice of meditation at eighteen, including two formative years of full time meditation and somatic regression practices in the Australian desert with her teacher, the modern mystic, Samuel Sagan.

Interspersed with thousands of hours of retreat practice throughout her twenties, she obtained an I.T. degree and pursued a demanding career in the growing field of digital technology.

The constant quest to integrate her spiritual experiences in everyday life and relationships invariably led her more deeply toward the pointings of non-dual Tantra and subsequently, all over the world, exploring the ancient temples and sacred sites of Indonesia, India and Egypt.

She currently resides in Ibiza, Spain, offering private sessions and sacred immersions.

Acknowledgements

To my father Alexandre Gonçalves for loving me so dearly and guiding me in so many ways, along many inspiring philosophical sojourns and for providing the unconditional love and acceptance that has watered my soul my entire life, I love you.

To my teacher Samuel Sagan; the non-dual pointings of Mark Whitwell, Mooji, and Amoda Maa; and the soul shaping poetry of Jallaluddin Rumi and Lal Ded.

To my dear friends Santosh Huot, Sofia Sundari and Lisa Harney for seeing me, walking the path beside me and lighting the way when I couldn't see myself.

To David Caddy of *Tears in the Fence*, David Brites, Ekaterina Dashkova and Clare Cowley for their reviews and persistent encouragement to complete this work.

To my mother, sister, family and dear friends who endlessly love and support me! I am beyond words with gratitude for how loved and blessed I am to have you in my life.

To the ones who took me to heaven, inspired me or helped the gods shake up my life on this earth, thank you for the teachings you unknowingly bestowed.

And finally, to He who appears in infinite forms, enchants me with wild devotion...

My great love, Shiva. The Lord of Innocence. To you I bow.

www.ingramcontent.com/pod-product-compliance
Lightning Source LLC
Chambersburg PA
CBHW020328010526
44107CB00054B/2017